THE LADYBIRD BOOK OF
BRITISH HISTORY

written by Tim Wood
Illustrated by Phil Page, John Dillow and Peter Dennis

Cover Illustration by Jim Eldridge
Design by Ali Stevenson
Consultants: School of History, University of Bristol
Illustrations on page 32 and page 56 by Anne Matthews
Additional research by Mike Gibson

A catalogue record for this book is available from the British Library
Published by Ladybird Books Ltd
80 Strand London WC2R 0RL
A Penguin Company
2 4 6 8 10 9 7 5 3
© Ladybird Books Ltd MMVII
LADYBIRD and the device of a Ladybird are trademarks of
Ladybird Books Ltd

ISBN: 978 1 84646 526 0
Printed in China

Contents

THE LADYBIRD BOOK OF

BRITISH HISTORY

The Romans

55 BC–AD 383

Britain before the Roman Invasion

About 2,700 years ago, people called Celts came to Britain from Europe. Gradually, they mixed in with the people who were already there. All those living in Britain became known as Britons. They were divided into groups called tribes.

The Romans Attack Britain, 55 BC

On a late summer morning in 55 BC, a Roman fleet appeared off the British coast near Dover. Consul Julius Caesar had brought an army of 10,000 men to see if Britain was worth invading. He also wanted to punish those British tribes who had been helping the Celts in Europe in their fight against the Romans.

At first the Romans were afraid of the thousands of British warriors waiting to fight them on the beach.

It was not until the standard bearer of the 10th legion jumped into the water that the rest of the Roman soldiers followed. The Britons fought desperately, but they were no match for the well trained Romans, and soon fled.

After his victory, Caesar left Britain. He returned with another army in the following year but left shortly after. The Romans did not return to Britain for another ninety-seven years.

Many British warriors painted or tattooed themselves with a blue dye called woad

Conquest, AD 43–AD 60

In AD 43, the Roman Emperor, Claudius, decided to make Britain part of the Roman Empire. An army of 40,000 Roman soldiers landed at Richborough in Kent. This time the Romans had come to stay.

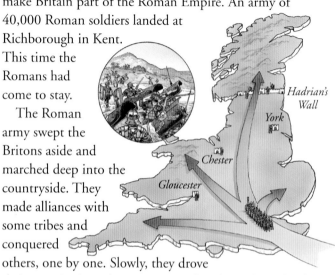

The Roman army swept the Britons aside and marched deep into the countryside. They made alliances with some tribes and conquered others, one by one. Slowly, they drove their enemies into the mountains of Wales and Scotland.

Scotland

The Romans did not invade Scotland until AD 84. Although they won some battles they could not conquer Scotland.

Captured

The chief enemy of Rome, Caratacus, king of the Catuvellauni tribe, fought the Romans in Wales. But he was betrayed by the queen of the Brigantes, captured and sent to Rome as a slave

The Roman Army

The Roman soldiers who invaded Britain were part of the best army in the world. They were better trained and armed than the wild Britons.

The Roman army was divided into legions, each one containing roughly 5,000 legionaries who signed up for twenty-five years. Each legionary was highly trained with daily sword practice and marching. Legionaries were also trained to build roads, bridges, forts and siege-engines.

A legionary wore heavy armour and had a large shield for protection. He carried two javelins and a short, sharp sword. Each legionary took food, cooking gear, an axe and two sharp stakes to help to build a wall round the camp at night.

A Roman legionary with his armour and equipment

Special Skills

Experienced officers were called centurions. They were in charge of a century, which was about eighty men.

The Roman army also contained many auxiliaries. These were soldiers from conquered tribes all over the Roman Empire. Some auxiliaries had special skills.

Archers *– many came from Syria. The Romans also used mounted archers*

Slingers *– many came from the Balearic Islands in the Mediterranean Sea*

*An experienced officer called a **centurion** was in charge of a century*

***Standard bearers** – each legion had its own standard called an eagle*

Battle

Legionaries were taught to fight in different formations. This usually gave them an advantage over their enemies who were not so well organised. In battle the whole army could fight as one man or split into smaller groups. Trumpets were used to give the signals.

Cohort *– about 480 soldiers. There were ten cohorts in a legion*

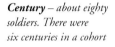

Century *– about eighty soldiers. There were six centuries in a cohort*

*The Romans locked their shields together to protect themselves from spears. The **cavalry** (mounted soldiers) would chase fleeing enemy soldiers during battle*

British Hill Forts

The British tribes had built many hill forts. To conquer Britain the Roman army had to capture these strongholds. Many had several ditches and walls round the hill top. A maze sometimes hid the main gate. The tribes lived in huts built inside the walls.

Boudicca's Revolt, AD 60

The fighting continued for almost twenty years after the Roman invasion. The Romans won many victories and it seemed as though nothing could stop them from ruling the whole country. Then in AD 60, the Iceni tribe, led by their queen, Boudicca, revolted.

Boudicca's army burned the Roman cities of Colchester...

St Albans...

and London.

They destroyed an entire legion.

Boudicca Meets Suetonius

1. Other tribes joined Boudicca and soon she had a huge army of 100,000 soldiers

2. Suetonius, the Roman Governor of Britain, was in Anglesey fighting the Druids. Hearing news of Boudicca's army, he marched quickly south-east with two legions to meet the Iceni

A great battle took place in the Midlands. Most of the British were killed and Boudicca herself took poison rather than be captured by the Romans. The rebellion was over.

The New Britons

After Boudicca's revolt, the Romans brought a new order to Britain. It became part of the Roman Empire and more Romans began to settle there. Latin became the main language for administration. Everyone had to obey Roman laws and follow the Roman way of life. Soon it was hard to tell who had been born in Britain and who was a foreigner. Romans became 'Roman Britons'.

The Romans built towns and cities which became centres of trade. Some Roman Britons grew wealthy by selling goods to the Romans. Roman governors were sent to rule Britain, and Britons had to pay taxes to Rome.

British nobles were trained to rule their tribes in the Roman way. This brought peace and riches to many, although some Britons who continued to fight against their new rulers were captured and became slaves. The Roman army built good roads so the legions could march quickly to any part of the country to keep the peace.

Hadrian's Wall

The Romans built forts in Wales and in the north of England to protect their land. The fierce, unconquered tribes hiding in the mountains and valleys of Scotland raided northern England again and again.

The emperor Hadrian decided to build a wall right across the country from Wallsend in Tyne and Wear to Bowness in Cumbria, to control them. The wall was finished in AD 128. It was 120 kilometres long and about four metres high, and was guarded by 15,000 Roman soldiers.

Every eight kilometres there was a large fort, which could hold up to 1,000 Roman soldiers. About every 1,500 metres there was a small fort called a milecastle, which could hold up to thirty soldiers. Between the milecastles were two turrets, which could shelter the sentries. Sentries guarded the wall all the time. If the tribes attacked, sentries ran for help or signalled with flags or fires.

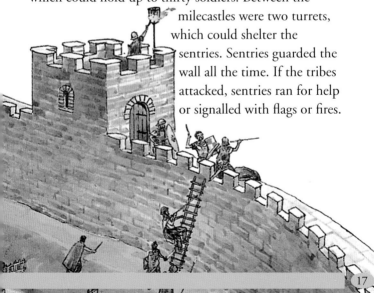

Roman Roads

The Romans built many roads. The legionaries did all the work: digging out the trenches, cutting the stones to shape and laying them. A curved surface and ditches at the side made sure that the rain ran off the road and did not wash away the stones.

Chalk, sand and broken brick

Roman surveyors used an instrument called a groma to get straight lines

Strong base of shaped stones

Chalk and sand

Roman Towns

From about AD 150 onwards, the Romans built walls round their towns to keep them safe from attack. Strongly built towns helped to keep peace and showed the Roman Britons how good Roman life could be. People came to the towns to buy and sell goods, to pay their taxes and to enjoy themselves.

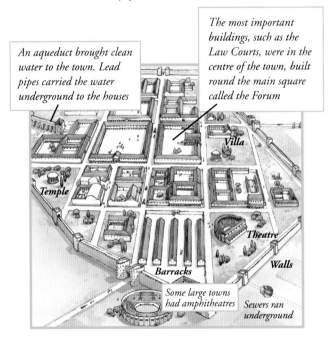

The most important buildings, such as the Law Courts, were in the centre of the town, built round the main square called the Forum

An aqueduct brought clean water to the town. Lead pipes carried the water underground to the houses

Villa

Temple

Theatre

Walls

Barracks

Some large towns had amphitheatres

Sewers ran underground

The streets were straight and laid out in the pattern of a chessboard. Some people lived in blocks of flats. Later, more comfortable houses were built

The Baths

Romans went to the baths to keep clean, relax, meet their friends and to exercise. Women and men bathed at separate times of the day.

Tepidarium – warm bath

Massage room

Food and wine were sold

Gymnasium – for exercise

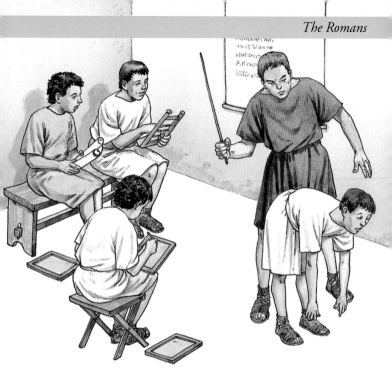

School

Only the children of rich parents went to school, starting at about the age of seven. They left primary school at the age of twelve. Boys went on to secondary school but girls, who were allowed to marry at the age of twelve, usually stopped going to school or had a home tutor.

The lessons were dull, with lots of copying and learning by heart. Schoolmasters were very strict and some beat their pupils.

What People Wore

Women wore sleeveless tunics made from linen or
cotton, or, if they were very rich, silk. They wore
coloured shawls over their tunics and as much
jewellery as they could afford.

*Female slaves wore
simple tunics*

Shawl

*Hairstyles were often
quite elaborate*

Most Romans wore boots or sandals

Men wore togas - loose robes made from the best wool if they were rich, or from coarse cloth if they were poor. Togas could be any colour but officials usually wore white togas decorated with a coloured stripe to show that the wearer was an important person.

Toga

Tunic

Slaves wore simple tunics made of coarse cloth or felt

Religion

The Romans brought their own religion to Britain. They worshipped many gods and goddesses in the new temples that they built. There was no special day for worship, so people went to the temple whenever they wanted and spoke to the god's statue to give thanks or to ask a favour.

Soon after the Roman invasion of Britain, Christianity began to spread throughout the Roman Empire. Many emperors tried to stop it, but they failed. In AD 313, Christianity became the religion of the whole Roman Empire.

The Romans Leave Britain

The Romans ruled Britain for over three hundred and fifty years. Many soldiers were needed to keep Britain safe. After AD 250, this task became harder, for several reasons.

Raiders from Scotland and Ireland began to make attacks on Britain. Saxon pirates made raids across the North Sea. The Roman forts on the south and east coasts could not keep them out.

The Roman Empire itself was being attacked by barbarians. Gradually, legions left Britain to defend other parts of the Empire. In AD 411, no more pay was sent from Rome and few Roman soldiers stayed after that.

The Britons were left to protect themselves from the new invaders. With the Romans gone there was no strong leader to rule the whole country and gradually the whole Roman way of life disappeared. Many people returned to the countryside and allowed the towns to fall into ruins.

THE LADYBIRD BOOK OF

BRITISH HISTORY

The Saxons, Vikings
and Normans

383–1272

Anglo-Saxon Settlers

In AD 407 British chiefs asked Anglo-Saxon soldiers to come from Germany to fight against the Picts and the Scots, fierce raiders from the North. In return for this help the Anglo-Saxons were given land. Some already lived in Britain and had fought in the Roman army.

The Anglo-Saxons were strong soldiers. They defeated the Picts and Scots and, when the Britons asked them to leave, they refused to go. As time passed, more and more Anglo-Saxons arrived, wanting land and attacking the Britons. Soon they began to settle in Britain. There were four main groups of German settlers – Angles, Saxons, Frisians and Jutes.

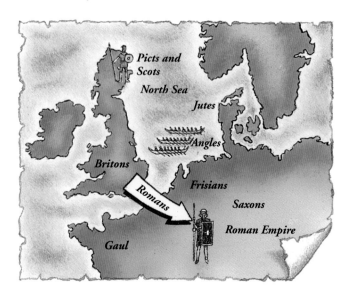

The Anglo-Saxons rowed across the North Sea in small boats. They fought the Britons and often won. Legend tells of a great British war leader who lived at this time and fought against the invaders. His name was Arthur.

Anglo-Saxon Villages

The Anglo-Saxon settlers rowed up the rivers looking for good places to build their villages. The best sites were easy to defend and had a good supply of water and wood. There were two or three large fields near each village where everyone helped to grow barley and wheat. The chief and the richer villagers lived in large houses. Poorer people lived in small houses built over pits in the ground. Some had wooden floorboards to keep the floor dry. People grew vegetables such as cabbages and onions, and they caught fish in the river. The villagers kept cattle, chickens, goats and pigs. They made the walls of their houses from split tree trunks, and they made thatched roofs from reeds or straw.

The Anglo-Saxon Kingdoms

For about one hundred and fifty years the Britons fought the Anglo-Saxons, but by the year 600 the Britons had either been forced to flee to Wales or the West Country or had become slaves.

By 600 Britain was divided into seven main Anglo-Saxon kingdoms: Northumbria, Mercia, Essex, East Anglia, Wessex, Kent and Sussex. They were often at war but no single kingdom was able to conquer the others. At first Kent was the most important. Two hundred years later, in 810, Wessex had become the most powerful.

How a Kingdom Was Organised

The **king** gave gifts of weapons and land to his people. In return they fought for him. He was advised by a council called the Witan.

The **thanes** were the nobles. They owned a lot of land and were expected to fight for the king. Some were made ealdormen and acted as judges and rulers in their areas.

The **churls** were free peasants who owned some land. They paid taxes and fought for their thane. They had to take part in village meetings called folk moots, which were held whenever there were arguments about the land.

Slaves could be bought, sold or given away. A slave could be worth as many as eight oxen. Many were British prisoners taken in battle, while others were born into slavery. Later Alfred, King of Wessex, passed laws allowing slaves to sell things they had made and to own some property.

Christianity

The Anglo-Saxons were pagans, who did not believe in the Christian God. There were still groups of Christians, some of whom were descended from the Roman Britons (Celts), living in parts of Ireland and Wales. Gradually these Celtic Christians returned to England and Scotland, and began to convert the Picts, Scots and Anglo-Saxons.

Over time, most of Britain became Christian. The Celtic Christians followed St Columba. The southern Christians followed St Augustine, from Rome. They argued about many things. A synod held in Whitby, Yorkshire, settled the arguments and in time the two groups of Christians united in the Roman Catholic Church.

Viking Raiders

In 789, more than three hundred years after the Anglo-Saxons had begun to settle in Britain, the first Viking raiders landed near Weymouth in Dorset.

They did little damage but a few years later more Vikings arrived. They attacked the monasteries at Lindisfarne and Jarrow, killing monks, stealing treasure from churches and capturing slaves.

The Vikings came from Norway, Sweden and Denmark. The winters there were long and cold, and the soil was poor. Britain was a rich prize for them.

A Viking longship carried about eighty men who rowed and sailed the ship and then fought on land using swords and battle axes.

The ships were strong enough to sail on rough seas and shallow enough to sail up rivers, deep into Britain. Soon Viking raids were happening almost every year.

In 851 a huge fleet of over three hundred and fifty Viking ships attacked the south of England and then, instead of sailing home across the North Sea, for the first time the raiders spent the winter in Kent.

Viking Settlers

About eighty years after their first attack, the Vikings formed a great army to conquer Britain and seven years later only the kingdom of Wessex remained free of them. When the Vikings took the Anglo-Saxon kingdom of Northumbria they made Jorvik (York) their capital.

Alfred the Great

In 871 Alfred became King of Wessex. The Vikings soon attacked his kingdom, but Alfred managed to escape and hid in the Athelney marshes in Somerset. He gathered an army and defeated the Viking king, Guthrum, at the battle of Edington, near Chippenham. The Vikings surrendered.

King Alfred and the Vikings made a treaty. The Vikings were to live in an area called the Danelaw, where they were allowed to follow Danish customs and obey the 'Danes' law'.

A statue of Alfred was put up in Winchester, Alfred's capital, in 1901

Alfred did not trust the Danes. He ordered ships and fortified towns called burhs to be built to protect England from possible Viking attack. He formed a new army called the fyrd.

Alfred's Laws

When Alfred became King of Wessex he introduced new laws. People who were accused of crimes had to appear in front of the village moot. If they did not appear they were declared outlaws and could be killed by anyone.

If accused people could not find enough oath-helpers (people who would swear they were innocent), they were 'tried by ordeal'. The Anglo-Saxons believed that God would judge whether the person was guilty or not. The accused person either picked a stone out of a pan of boiling water or carried a bar of red-hot iron for several paces. If the scalded or burned hand had begun to heal after three days the person was innocent. If not, he or she was guilty.

Sports and Pastimes

During the time that the Anglo-Saxons and the Danes lived in their separate kingdoms there were problems, quarrels and wars but in times of peace both groups enjoyed themselves.

The Danes enjoyed sports like weightlifting using heavy boulders, which showed off their strength. They also enjoyed board games. Viking poets recited poems called sagas, which told of the adventures and brave deeds of heroes and gods.

Slaves served the food

The Anglo-Saxons and the Vikings loved feasting. The guests ate large amounts of roast and boiled meat with bread, peas and cabbage. This food was washed down with vast quantities of beer, wine and mead.

England after Alfred

Within thirty years of Alfred's death, England had become a united country. There were three kings who helped to make the peace. Alfred's son, Edward, and grandson, Athelstan, conquered Danelaw. A few years later, Viking raids from Ireland and Norway were defeated, and Athelstan made peace with the Welsh and the Northumbrians.

King Edgar encouraged the building of many new monasteries and, at the end of his reign in 975, most of England was peaceful and prosperous.

Danegeld

In 980 Danish raids on England began again. The king, Ethelred, was not able to defeat the invaders so he paid them large amounts of silver and gold to go.

This money (called Danegeld) simply made the Danes eager for more and they returned in greater numbers. Within forty years, they had conquered the Anglo-Saxons and King Sweyn of Denmark became the first Danish king of England.

King Cnut was Sweyn's son and he took the English throne after his father. In spite of the fears of the Anglo-Saxons, he was a very fair king. His two sons followed him on the throne. Then, when the second son died, Ethelred's son, Edward, returned from France to become king of England.

Struggle for the Throne

Edward rebuilt Westminster Abbey and was later known as 'the Confessor' which means 'strong believer in Christianity'. Edward died without a son to follow him. Three men each claimed the right to be the next king: William, Duke of Normandy; Harald Hardrada, King of Norway and Harold, Earl of Wessex.

First, Harold of Wessex was crowned in January 1066. Then William, feeling cheated, gathered an army to invade England. The ships were delayed by bad weather. Meanwhile, Harald of Norway invaded northern England in September. Harold marched north and defeated Harald at the battle of Stamford Bridge. A few days later, William's fleet landed near Hastings. He waited for Harold. Harold marched south, not waiting to gather a larger army.

The Battle of Hastings

The battle began at nine o' clock in the morning on 14th October 1066. The English locked their shields together to make a wall and defended the top of a hill with axes and swords.

The Normans, most of whom were trained knights on horses, charged up the hill all morning but could not break through the shield wall. However, many of the English left the safety of the shield wall to chase the Norman knights and were killed. Gradually the English army began to break up.

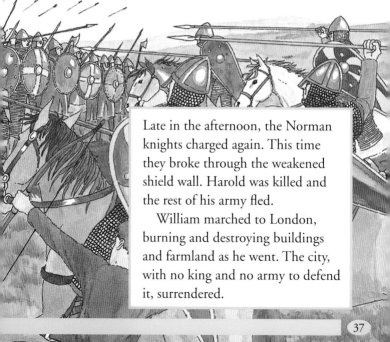

Late in the afternoon, the Norman knights charged again. This time they broke through the weakened shield wall. Harold was killed and the rest of his army fled.

William marched to London, burning and destroying buildings and farmland as he went. The city, with no king and no army to defend it, surrendered.

Norman Castles

William was crowned King of England on Christmas Day 1066, and for the next 100 years England was ruled by the Normans. There were over two million Anglo-Saxons in England and only ten thousand Norman knights. To make it easier to control the people, William and the barons built castles all over the country.

Kings and Tenants

William gave his supporters land on condition that they fought for him. This is known as feudalism.

The king

How Feudalism Worked

Land was given to tenants-in-chief, who were mostly Norman church leaders and barons. They provided soldiers and paid taxes to the king. They divided their land into smaller areas called fees (fiefs) and allowed tenants to live on them. A tenant swore loyalty to his baron. Tenants provided soldiers and paid taxes to the barons. In turn, they were allowed to work on the land. Peasants were allowed to work on the land provided they also worked for the tenants and paid them taxes.

A soldier

A peasant

The Domesday Book

William wanted to find out how much his land was
worth so that he could work out what taxes everyone
should pay. He sent teams of officials to every corner of
the country to find out about his new kingdom. They
asked questions in every village and the answers were later
written down in two volumes called the Domesday Book.
'Domesday' means 'The Day of Judgement'.

Some of the questions which were asked for the Domesday Book:

How many ploughs are there?
How much land is good for growing crops?
How much is just wasteland?
How much is the land worth?

The Crusades

William's descendants, especially Henry II, the first
Plantagenet king, gained a huge empire in France.
However Henry's son, King Richard I, was more
interested in fighting in the Holy Land. In about 1070
the Turks had captured the Holy Land and had stopped
Christian travellers from visiting the holy places where
Jesus had lived. The Pope ordered all Christians to
recapture the Holy Land. Knights from all over Europe
answered his call but it was not until 1190 that English
knights were led on a crusade by their king, Richard I.

What People Wore

Fashions changed greatly during the time of the Anglo-Saxons, the Vikings and the Normans. Most clothes were made of wool or linen, dyed with vegetable dyes.

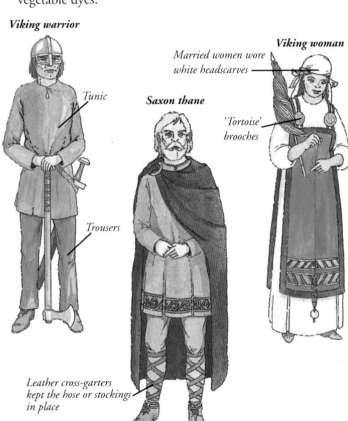

Viking warrior

Tunic

Trousers

Leather cross-garters kept the hose or stockings in place

Saxon thane

Viking woman

Married women wore white headscarves

'Tortoise' brooches

Men's cloaks were usually fastened on the right
shoulder to leave the sword arm free. When fighting,
knights wore armour, made of iron rings sewn onto
a leather coat called a hauberk.

Norman knight

Hauberk – slit for
horseriding

Kite-shaped
shield

Spurs

Chausses

Norman baron

Hair shaved
at the back

Over tunic

Under tunic

Leather
shoes

Norman lady

Over tunic –
laced at
the sides

Outer
tunic

Inner
tunic

Saxon woman

The Magna Carta

The Norman barons, who owned lands in England and France, used their great riches to build strong castles. By 1215 a number of the barons had banded together and become so powerful that they forced King John to grant the Magna Carta (Great Charter). This was partly an agreement that the king should not tax the barons unfairly, but it also gave details about how the kingdom should be ruled justly.

Simon de Montfort

Under Henry III, who came to the throne in 1216 at the age of nine, a group of barons, led by Simon de Montfort, Earl of Leicester, became very powerful. At one point they actually ruled England in place of the king. De Montfort called on the help of knights and important citizens to rule England. This was a significant step in the development of parliament.

THE LADYBIRD BOOK OF

BRITISH
HISTORY

The Middle Ages

1272–1485

The Manor

In the Middle Ages almost everyone lived in a village like this. The baron (lord of the manor) owned all the land and most villagers were not allowed to leave it without his permission.

The lord of the manor allowed the villagers to farm some of his land. In return they had to work for him during the week and pay him with crops and animals.

Most villages were surrounded by three huge fields which were divided by banks of earth into long, thin strips. Each villager farmed some strips in each field, so the good and bad land was shared out fairly.

A lord usually owned several manors. He visited each in turn, taking his family, servants and most of his possessions with him. When the lord was away the bailiff was left in charge.

Villagers gathered wood, berries and nuts from the forest and grazed their animals on the common land, which they shared. They had everything they needed except salt and iron, which they had to buy from the nearest town.

Every year the reeve (who organised the villagers' work) and the villagers decided what to grow. One field was used as a pasture for animals. The second was sown with wheat (for bread) and the third with barley (for beer). All the villagers helped, including the children. Most of the work was done by hand, although there were oxen to help to pull heavy loads or to plough.

Peasants lived in wooden huts with roofs made of thatch. The family lived in one end, animals in the other. The huts were dirty, smelly and dark.

Food

The main food for a peasant family was bread. Some peasants kept chickens, pigs and cows. Water was not clean, so often people drank beer. During a long winter many peasants went hungry and some starved.

The lord of the manor ate fresh food all year round. He kept doves and tame rabbits. He could hunt wild boar or stags in the forest, or go hawking. Peasants were not allowed to hunt, and any caught doing so could be punished or even hanged.

On feast days the lord of the manor held a banquet in the Great Hall of his manor house or castle. It could last up to five hours with as many as forty different dishes.

The lord of the manor and his special guests sat at the high table. Jesters, acrobats and tumblers entertained the feasters

Towns

Around sixty million people live in Britain today. In the Middle Ages the population was much smaller (three to six million). Towns were small and the largest city was London. In the year 1300 only 60,000 people lived in the city, compared with about seven million today.

Fire was a great danger in the towns, where wooden houses and workshops were crammed closely together. People threw their rubbish straight out of the windows so the narrow streets were dirty, smelly and often swarming with rats and flies.

Guilds were clubs started by the most skilled of all the workers, the master craftsmen. Each trade had its own guild and only guild members were allowed to make and sell those goods in the town.

Becoming a master craftsman

1. Apprentice for seven years. Apprentices slept in the workshop and were paid nothing
2. Journeyman for several years. Received pay
3. Produced a masterpiece as a test. If it was good enough, he was taken into the guild and could open his own shop

Monasteries

Monks and nuns spent their lives cut off from the rest of the world in monasteries or nunneries. Although they spent most of their time praying, many also farmed the land around the monasteries. They allowed travellers to stay free for two nights and ran hospitals for the poor. They kept dole cupboards, inside which they left bread and drink for the poor.

The monastery would cover a large area and would include farmland, a guesthouse, a brewery, a hospital and a bakehouse.

Pilgrims

People who had done something wrong and wanted to be forgiven often went on a pilgrimage to pray at a shrine. Some pilgrims went abroad to places like Assisi or Rome in Italy, or even as far as Jerusalem in the Holy Land. The journey was very exciting and sometimes dangerous, with strange places to visit and new people to meet. A pilgrimage was the only chance for rich and poor people to meet as equals.

Knights

Knights were landowners who had been given land as a reward for fighting for the king or baron. They could be asked to spend up to forty days each year serving in the king's army. A boy from a wealthy family would train for up to ten years to become a knight, by serving first as a page and then as a squire. As a squire, he looked after the knight's armour and helped him to dress for battle. He learned how to ride and how to fight.

Tournaments were held so that knights could practise jousting. Crowds of people came to watch. Each knight tried to knock the other off his horse. They were allowed three lances. When these had been broken the fight continued on foot. A defeated knight gave up his horse and armour. Jousting was dangerous and knights were often injured or killed.

Today some people believe that knights had to be hoisted onto their saddles. This actually never happened

Lance

Castles

Kings and barons built castles to protect their lands. After defeating the Welsh, Edward I of England built many castles in Wales to control the country. Other castles were built in the north of England as protection against Scottish raiders.

1. *Ladder*
2. *Mantlet – protective screen let archers move closer to the walls*
3. *Battering ram*
4. *Belfry – movable tower covered in wet animal hides to make it harder to burn*
5. *Hoarding – overhanging gallery gave cover for defenders*

The increasing use of gunpowder and cannons meant that, after 1350, fewer castles were built.

6. *Mine – tunnel dug under wall, filled with wood and then set on fire to make wall collapse*
7. *Mangonel – twisted ropes provided the power for this catapult to hurl stones*
8. *Arrow slits – specially shaped to give defenders a good view and to give attackers a very small target*
9. *Hot pitch, oil, water or sand were poured down*

The Hundred Years War

During the Middle Ages, parts of France were ruled by the English and parts by the French. Each side wanted the land owned by the other. The war which broke out between them in 1337 lasted until 1453 and is known as the Hundred Years War.

The Battle of Agincourt took place on 25th October 1415. The French had high hopes of winning. Reports said they had 50,000 men whilst the English, led by Henry V, had only 6,000. The French had chosen the site carefully but as their first line of attack charged they were caught in a field of mud caused by rain the night before.

It was the skill of the English archers that won the battle. Their steel-tipped arrows could kill an armoured knight at two hundred paces. A skilled archer could fire twelve arrows a minute. After three hours, the English won the battle. However, they could not win the war.

Medicine

People in the Middle Ages did not live as long as people do today. Most died before the age of fifty. Doctors were not allowed to cut up dead people to find out what caused disease, so they knew little about curing sickness.

Doctors believed that illness was often caused by 'badness' in the blood. Sometimes they would cut a vein to let some of this 'bad' blood out. They also

sometimes used worms called leeches to suck out patients' blood.

Physicians used astrological charts, herbs, spells and charms as cures. Some prepared ointments made from animal fat, blood or dung. Most of their cures were useless.

Surgeons were barbers who also pulled out teeth and did small operations. Their shops had red and white striped poles outside to show the blood and bandages of their trade. These red and white signs are still sometimes used today.

Manuscripts from the 13th century show that medieval brain operations were carried out. Anaesthetics for stopping pain did not exist then, so patients would have suffered terrible pain and probably died soon after.

The Black Death

In 1348 a terrible plague reached England. It came from China, carried on the fleas which lived on black rats. People bitten by these fleas developed lumps as big as apples in their armpits, followed by the red and black spots which gave the disease its name, the Black Death.

Black rats lived in the holds of ships and carried the plague from China

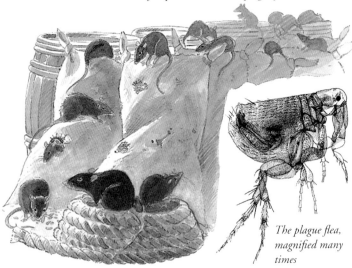

The plague flea, magnified many times

Doctors did not understand what caused the Black Death, and there was no cure. Within two years the plague had killed one-third of the population.

Doctors wore strange outfits with a mask and a special beak that was stuffed with herbs. They thought this would help protect them from the disease. Others would carry a pomander stuffed with herbs, held to their nose.

There were so many deaths from the plague that the dead bodies would be collected on carts and buried together in large graves. At one point, in the biggest cities, there were barely enough living people left to bury the dead.

Whole households were affected by the illness. Whole villages were even abandoned because of the plague. The traces of these 'ghost villages' can still be seen in the countryside today, from the crop-marks in the fields. The disease also halted Edward III's campaign against Scotland, which delighted the Scots. However, soon enough the plague struck there too.

The Black Death lasted on and off for over 150 years, but Scotland, Ireland and Wales were never affected as badly as England. It wasn't until 1894 that a medical scientist actually discovered what had caused the plague. Before then, nobody knew that it was caused by the fleas on the rats.

What People Wore

Poor people wore cheap, rough, woollen clothes. Rich people wore finer woollen clothes decorated with fur and jewellery. Towards the end of the period women's hats and hairstyles became very grand, and rich people wore lots of decoration such as embroidery on their clothing. Townspeople copied the styles of the rich, but they used cheaper materials.

Sport

Medieval people played many of the sports we play today, but the games were more violent. Football was played between all the men of two villages. The ball was a pig's bladder stuffed with peas and the aim of the game was to carry it across the fields and place it on the market cross of the other village. There were no rules, so players were often hurt and sometimes even killed. King Edward III banned the game because he thought that people were more interested in playing football than practising their archery.

Other sports and pastimes included bear baiting (where a chained bear was attacked by dogs), cock fighting, skittles, wrestling and shin kicking.

1. Cockfighting
*2. Bear baiting -
a chained bear was
attacked by dogs*
3. Archery

The Peasants' Revolt

After the Black Death there were fewer peasants to farm the land. The overworked survivors grew to hate their manor duties. They wanted to be paid wages and to be free to leave the manor. They were angry when a law was passed to stop this.

In 1381 King Richard brought in a poll tax to pay for the war against France. Everyone over the age of fifteen, rich or poor, had to pay one shilling, a large sum of money in those days.

The peasants attacked their lords. John Ball, a poor priest, encouraged the men of Kent to march to London to try to get higher wages and freedom. Young King Richard, who was only fourteen at the time, met the peasants. Their leader, Wat Tyler, was killed by the Lord Mayor of London.

The king promised to help, but when the peasants returned home their leaders were hanged. However, no more poll taxes were introduced and in time wages began to rise.

THE LADYBIRD BOOK OF

BRITISH
HISTORY

The Tudors

1485–1603

A New Age Begins

Henry Tudor defeated King Richard III at the battle of
Bosworth Field in 1485. When Richard was killed in
the fight his crown was plucked from a bush and placed
on Henry's head. Richard's death ended the Wars of the
Roses between the Yorkists and Lancastrians, members of
the royal family who had been struggling for the throne
for thirty years.

Henry being crowned

The new king, Henry VII, was a Lancastrian. He made
his claim to the throne stronger by marrying Elizabeth
of York, his fourth cousin and a member of the Yorkists.
Henry had lived abroad so the English people knew
nothing of him and could never have imagined that his
family was going to rule England for the next 120 years.

Henry brought peace to the country but he did not feel completely safe on the throne. He believed that to be a strong king he needed to have plenty of money. He told his servants to collect as much money for him as they could. Then he made sure that he did not have to spend this money on wars because they were too expensive.

Henry became a rich man. Although not a popular king, he was respected. When he died in 1509 he passed a safe and strong crown to his son, Henry VIII. When Henry VIII came to the throne however, he spent all the money his father had made in fighting wars against France.

Henry VIII had to put down two rebellions by men claiming his throne. One rebel, Lambert Simnel, was only thirteen years old. After beating his rebel army Henry put Simnel to work in the royal kitchens. The other rebel, Perkin Warbeck, was trained by his tutor to pretend to be Richard, Duke of York, a member of the royal family. He was also captured and Henry had him executed.

Lambert Simnel

Henry VIII and His Wives

Two weeks after Henry VIII was crowned, he married Catherine of Aragon, a Spanish princess. Although she was a good wife to him, she did not have any sons. Henry thought that England would be weak if there was no king to follow him.

Henry asked the Pope to give him a divorce so that he could marry again. The Pope refused, so Henry broke away from the Catholic church and set up his own Church of England. He divorced Catherine and married Anne Boleyn, a lady-in-waiting. Anne did not have a son either and when Henry tired of her, he had her executed.

Henry's third wife, Jane Seymour, did give him a son, Edward, but she died twelve days later. Henry then married Anne of Cleves. She had no children and Henry divorced her. Next he married Catherine Howard, whom he later had executed. His last wife was Catherine Parr who was lucky enough to outlive him.

After Henry had made himself head of the new Church of England, he began to close the monasteries. Many monks had never accepted the new religion and Henry did not trust them because they still thought of the Pope as their leader.

As a young king Henry was tall, handsome and intelligent. He was interested in music, books and sport. He had several magnificent palaces where he lived with his courtiers. They dressed in their finest clothes and jewels, and were entertained with dancing, poetry readings and music. Outside, in the royal gardens and forests, all kinds of sport were played.

Henry sent his chief minister to investigate the monasteries

Edward VI, the Boy King

When Henry VIII died in 1547 his only son, Edward, became king. Edward was just nine years old so first his uncle, the Duke of Somerset, and then the Duke of Northumberland ruled England in his name. Edward was never in good health and died at the age of fifteen.

Henry VIII had closed the monastery schools. During Edward's reign new grammar schools were started to teach boys to read and write. Schoolteachers were very strict and beat their pupils with birches if they misbehaved. The most important subject was Latin. Although letters were written in English, most important books were written in Latin. Pupils used goosefeather quills for writing. They had to sharpen the quills and mix their own ink.

Changes in the Countryside

By Tudor times landowners had found that they could make more money by raising sheep for the wool trade than by growing corn to make bread. Since it was easier to look after sheep in an enclosed space, they began to plant hedges to make smaller fields. Soon much of the land, including the commons, had been enclosed.

Many peasants kept bees. Using honey was the only way the Tudors had of sweetening their food

Without the common land, the peasants could no longer grow enough food for themselves. Even worse, many of them lost their jobs because sheep did not need so many people to look after them. The difficulties were even greater because the population had grown so fast that there was not enough bread to feed them.

Many peasants were so angry about the enclosures that they tore down the hedges and demanded that land should be ploughed for corn. In 1549 peasants in the eastern counties rebelled, protesting about enclosures, high rents and low wages. Their leader Robert Ket and about fifty others were hanged.

Bloody Mary

Before Edward VI died his ministers had persuaded him to make a will naming Lady Jane Grey as queen. They wanted her because, although her claim to the throne was only slight, she was a Protestant. But Mary, Henry VIII's elder daughter, came to London to claim the throne. Lady Jane was arrested and later executed. She was just seventeen years old.

Mary married King Philip II of Spain. The marriage made her very unpopular because people feared that Spaniards would rule England.

Mary was a strong Catholic and when she became queen she was determined that England should return to the old religion. Nearly 300 people who refused to give up the Protestant faith were burned at the stake.

Bishops Latimer and Ridley being burned at the stake in Oxford. It was believed that although the body was burned, the soul of the victim would go to Heaven

A New Queen

In 1558 Mary died and her sister Elizabeth became
queen. The new queen faced many problems. She
was short of money and England was threatened by
Scotland, France and Spain.

Elizabeth was a Protestant but she tried to make the
Church of England acceptable to Catholics. Elizabeth
was an intelligent, courageous and determined woman.
She was also very popular with the people of England
and became a much loved and respected ruler,
known as Good Queen Bess.

*The Elizabethan Age began with Elizabeth's coronation. The crowds
fought to cut little pieces off the blue carpet on which she walked, to keep
as souvenirs*

Tudor Houses

Some people became very rich in Elizabeth's reign. They built houses that were a lot more comfortable than medieval houses had been. Many houses were built with a timber frame filled in with plaster. Magnificent houses were built by rich nobles, often in the shape of an E for Elizabeth.

Poor people lived in much smaller houses

Beggars

During Elizabeth's reign there was a great increase in the number of poor people. This was partly because the population rose, but also because enclosures meant that there were fewer jobs so many people could not afford the high food prices.

In years when the harvest failed and food was short, people went hungry. They were forced to travel to look for food or charity. Beggars were very skilful at making people feel sorry for them so that they would give more money. Some pretended to be horribly injured, while others pretended to be mad. Some would eat soap to make themselves froth at the mouth.

They were often joined by soldiers returning from wars abroad. Large groups of these beggars brought terror to whole towns as they attacked and robbed the townspeople. These beggars were punished in houses of correction by being whipped, or branded with hot irons.

Crime and Punishment

There was a lot of crime in Tudor times. There was no paid police force so people had to look for the criminals themselves. Those who were caught were punished very harshly as an example to others. People could be hanged for stealing.

The gallows*. Common people were hanged. Nobles were usually beheaded*

Punishment for minor crimes

The stocks

Whipping

The crimes of treason, rebellion, riot, murder and most kinds of stealing were all punished by death. Since modern police methods such as fingerprinting had not been invented, it was hard to prove a criminal was guilty so people were sometimes made to confess to crimes by torture.

The rack was a widely used instrument of torture

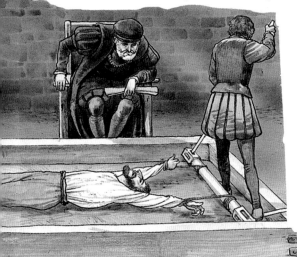

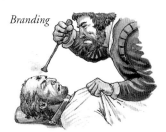

Branding

Pillory

Sports and Pastimes

Hunting for stags, deer and hares was very popular among landowners. Hunt picnics were arranged in the forests. The Elizabethans were very fond of dancing. In one dance, the volta, ladies jumped high in the air. Some people thought it disgraceful because the ladies showed their knees. In Tudor times there were few story books but poetry was very popular. The theatre was also very well-loved and William Shakespeare's plays were among those performed at the new theatres.

What People Wore

At the time of Henry VII men wore jackets called doublets and woollen tights called hose. Ladies wore velvet gowns and headdresses. In Elizabethan times ladies wore corsets stiffened with wood or iron, starched collars called ruffs and skirts supported by wooden hoops. Men wore short padded trousers called breeches.

Mary, Queen of Scots

Mary, Queen of Scots was a rival to Elizabeth. She was Elizabeth's cousin and would become queen if Elizabeth died without having any children. Mary fled to England to seek Elizabeth's protection after a rebellion of the Scottish lords in 1568.

Mary was also a Catholic and many Catholics felt that she should be queen instead of Elizabeth. For nineteen years Mary was imprisoned in various English castles.

Foolishly, she became involved in Catholic plots against Elizabeth. When proof of Mary's plotting was given to the queen, she signed Mary's death warrant with sadness. Mary was executed at Fotheringay Castle in 1587.

Sea Dogs

In 1492 Christopher Columbus discovered America for the king of Spain. The Spanish conquered the Aztecs and Incas who lived there, and took their land and wealth. Spanish treasure fleets, loaded with gold and silver, sailed across the Atlantic to land their cargoes in Spain. Spain became the richest country in Europe.

Elizabeth encouraged English sea captains, nicknamed 'sea dogs', to attack the slow Spanish galleons and steal their treasure. To the Spanish king, Philip II, the sea dogs were little better than pirates. To the English, they became heroes.

Francis Drake was the first English sea captain to sail around the world. He attacked Spanish ports in America and stole over £1,500,000 of gold. The Spanish called him 'el draco' – the dragon.

A Spanish galleon

The Armada

King Philip II became more and more angry with
Elizabeth over the sea dogs, and also because she was
helping Dutch Protestant rebels who were fighting
against Spain.

Philip was a strong Catholic and he wanted England
to be a Catholic country. He plotted to put Mary, Queen
of Scots on the throne of England but she was executed
in 1587. The following year Philip decided to take action
and sent a great fleet, or Armada, of 130 ships carrying
30,000 soldiers and sailors to invade England.

Beacon fires were lit across England to spread the news
of the Armada's arrival. In spite of English attacks in the
channel, the Armada reached Calais safely. The English
sent fireships into the Spanish fleet and it scattered in
panic. A great storm blew up, driving the Spanish ships
northwards. They had to sail right round Scotland. Many
were wrecked and less than half of the Spanish ships
managed to limp back to Spain. The Armada had failed.

The Death of the Queen

On Thursday 24th March 1603 a hush fell over London. Good Queen Bess had died, aged nearly seventy. Elizabeth had never married, and she had no children to follow her. She was the last Tudor ruler.

Few of her subjects remembered what it was like to be ruled by a king. She had shown that a woman could rule as well as any man. Though she had become less popular in her later years, her reign had been one of the most glorious in English history.

Elizabeth's funeral

As soon as Elizabeth died, a messenger rode north to tell King James VI of Scotland, the son of Mary, Queen of Scots, that he was to be crowned James I of England. He was the first of a new family of rulers – the Stuarts.

THE LADYBIRD BOOK OF

BRITISH

HISTORY

The Stuarts

1603–1714

King James I (James VI of Scotland)

James believed that he was king by God's will and he expected Parliament to obey him without question. He entertained so magnificently that he was often short of money. When the MPs refused to vote him any he dismissed Parliament and raised cash by other means, such as selling land and titles to his friends.

James ordered scholars to prepare a new translation of the Bible. The King James Bible was produced in 1611. It stayed the same for 300 years and can still be bought today.

In Stuart times people smoked using clay pipes. James hated smoking and wrote a book in 1604 setting out his arguments against it.

James was clever and well-educated but he was not

popular. He was said to be clumsy and he even fell down at his own coronation. During his reign two problems which had been simmering during the Elizabethan Age boiled to the surface. These were the power of Parliament and problems of religion.

James going to Parliament

The Gunpowder Plot

Soon after James came to the throne, a group of Roman Catholic nobles plotted to blow up Parliament. They were angry because James had ordered all Catholic priests to leave the country, and would not allow Catholics to worship as they pleased. They chose a time when the king, the queen and many important nobles and church leaders would be there.

In the early hours of the morning of 5th November 1605 a Catholic soldier, Guy Fawkes, was arrested in a cellar under the House of Lords. He was carrying some matches. Searchers found a tunnel leading from the house next door, and thirty-six barrels of gunpowder hidden under a pile of wood in the cellar. Several other plotters were arrested later. They were all hung, drawn and quartered.

Some historians believe that the king's minister, Robert Cecil, may have known about the plot for a long time. He may have allowed it to go on so that he could catch all the plotters or to make Catholics unpopular throughout the country.

Guy Fawkes

The Pilgrim Fathers

Like the Catholics, the Puritans were not allowed to worship as they wished. In 1620 some of them decided to sail across the Atlantic and set up home in America.

One hundred men, women and children set out in a ship called the *Mayflower*. After a stormy voyage lasting sixty-seven days, they landed in America. Although half of them died during the hard winter, the rest survived to build a town and start farms. Friendly native tribesmen taught them about local plants and seeds.

Charles I

In 1625 James died and his son Charles became king. The new king soon quarrelled with Parliament, mainly about money and religion. Charles also believed that he was king by God's will, just as his father had. Parliament tried to use his need for money to control his power. In 1629 Charles decided to rule without Parliament but his new taxes made him unpopular. In addition, many people feared that Charles would bring back the Roman Catholic religion. In 1640 Charles, who needed money to fight a war against the Scots, recalled Parliament. MPs, led by John Pym, began to pass laws to control the king. One law said that Parliament could not be dismissed without its own agreement.

In 1642 Charles declared war on the Parliamentarians. He left London and headed north to raise an army, calling on all loyal people to support him. Parliament asked its followers to oppose the king. The Civil War had begun.

The Start of the Civil War

When the Civil War began, people had to choose sides.
Sometimes families were divided in their loyalties, with
relations fighting on opposite sides. Officers in the king's
army were called Cavaliers. They had long hair and
dressed in fine clothes. Soldiers in the Parliament's army
were called Roundheads because of their close-cropped
hair and round helmets.

Supporters of the king:
Great landowners
Catholics
*People in the north
and west of the country*

Supporters of Parliament:
*Centres of trade and wealth,
such as London*
*Large towns and seaports,
whose people hated the
king's taxes*
*Puritans and those who
feared the king would bring
back the Catholic religion*

Marston
Moor

Preston

Naseby

Worcester

Oxford London

Bristol
Lansdown

Newbury

The Triumph of Parliament

After several defeats Parliament appointed a brilliant army
captain, Oliver Cromwell, to train its soldiers. He created
a 'New Model Army' which crushed the king's army at
the battle of Naseby. The lightly armoured and poorly
disciplined Royalist forces stood little chance against the
New Model Army whose cavalrymen often wore armour
and fought with swords or pistols and muskets.

After losing the key towns of Bristol and Oxford, Charles
surrendered. Parliament could not decide what to do with
him. In 1648 Charles escaped from London and tried to
restart the war.

Cromwell believed that as long as Charles lived, there
would never be peace in the land. He decided to arrest
the king and put him on trial for treason.

The Execution of the King

In 1649 the real power in the country was the army. MPs who still wished to make a pact with the king were driven out of Parliament. Those who remained prepared for the king's trial in Westminster Hall.

Throughout his trial Charles behaved with great dignity. He refused to accept that the court had any right to try him. He was called a tyrant, a traitor and a murderer and sentenced to death.

It was a freezing day in January when Charles went to the scaffold. He wore an extra shirt so that he would not shiver and seem afraid. After making a short speech he laid his head on the block. A loud groan rose from the crowd as the executioner's axe came down.

The Commonwealth

After the execution of the king Britain became a republic, called the Commonwealth, ruled by Cromwell and Parliament. However, when Parliament would not agree to new elections Cromwell, backed by the army, dismissed the MPs. He ruled, as Lord Protector, himself.

Cromwell was a Puritan. He passed laws against swearing, dancing, card playing and football. Theatres and inns were closed, and at one stage even Christmas dinner was forbidden. Many people hated these laws and longed for a return to things as they used to be. Puritans believed in a simple life and hard work.

When Cromwell died in 1658 his son, Richard, became Lord Protector. He was disliked by the army and soon retired. An army officer, General Monck, who realised that Britain needed a ruler invited Charles I's son to return from abroad to become King Charles II.

Charles II loved dancing and the theatre and many other things the Puritans had outlawed. He became known as 'the Merry Monarch'.

The Great Plague

The summer of 1665 was unusually hot. During June a terrible plague struck London, killing 68,000, a quarter of the people who lived there. The filthy, narrow streets provided perfect conditions for the rats to breed and for the disease to spread. Carters toured the streets ringing bells and shouting 'Bring out your dead'. They took the corpses out of the town, buried them in a pit and covered them with quicklime.

Red crosses were painted on the doors of houses which had been visited by the plague. The people inside were not allowed to come out. Sometimes food was left for them on the doorstep.

There was no cure for the plague. Some people thought it was caused by foul air so fires were lit in the streets to drive it away. Many people fled to the countryside to escape.

The Great Fire of London

In the year following the plague, a second disaster struck London. A fire broke out in a baker's shop in Pudding Lane. Fanned by a strong wind, the flames spread quickly through the narrow streets of wooden houses. Many people panicked and, grabbing what belongings they could carry, fled for the river Thames.

The king ordered sailors to blow up houses with gunpowder in order to make an open space across which the fire could not cross. But it was not until the fifth day of the fire, when the wind changed direction, that the flames were at last brought under control. Much of London was left a charred and smoking ruin.

Sir Christopher Wren

So much of London had been destroyed by the Great Fire that the king called on an architect, Christopher Wren, to design a new city. He made sure that all buildings in the city were built of brick or stone and that roads were made wider. Wren rebuilt fifty-one churches, but St Paul's Cathedral was his masterpiece. It took thirty-seven years to build. Wren was buried there when he died aged ninety.

Daily Life

The food most people ate was bread, cheese, cheap cuts of meat and beer. Wealthy people ate huge amounts of meat, poultry and fish. Increasing trade with overseas countries brought new kinds of food from abroad, such as tomatoes, pineapples and chocolate. Coffee was popular and a new, very expensive drink called tea.

The houses of rich nobles or merchants were built of stone or brick with sash windows and a regular shape. Bathrooms were starting to appear by the end of the era.

During the early Stuart period, fashions became more colourful and lost the padded stiffness of the Elizabethan age. Ribbons became popular decorations. Then, during the Commonwealth, fashions became simpler, because most forms of decoration were banned. When Charles II became king, colour and decoration returned.

Cavalier about 1630

Lady about 1645

Mask – to protect skin from the sun

Breeches below the knee

Most people still worked on the land in Stuart times, but industry was becoming more important. Wool was spun and woven in most country cottages. Merchants called clothiers bought the wool, took it to the cottages and paid for the finished cloth.

The fastest growing industry was coal. Coal was carried by sea from Newcastle to heat homes in London. Hundreds of small boys worked in the capital climbing and sweeping chimneys. The iron industry, glass making and salt mining were also important. Ships built in ports like Newcastle and Bristol carried the goods overseas.

Silk overdress

Full wig

Lady about 1690

Gentleman about 1690

Witchcraft

In Stuart times people believed that witches were working with the devil to try to harm good people. If someone died or a cow became sick for no apparent reason, it was easy to blame a witch.

Suspected witches were often 'floated' by being lowered into water. If they floated, they were witches. If they sank, they were innocent but probably died by drowning! Most people were so frightened by being arrested that they 'confessed' and often gave away others. Witches were hanged. We will never know how many innocent people, mostly old women, died for the sake of this terrible superstition. People with pets were instantly suspected because witches were thought to keep their own evil spirit in an animal called a familiar, which they fed on their blood. Witch finders looked for a strange mark on the body from which the familiar drank blood.

Science

Before the Stuart period little was known about science and a great deal of what was known was based on superstition or guesswork. During James I's reign Roger Bacon began to carry out scientific experiments to discover more about the world. Roger Bacon's ideas about the importance of experiments were continued by scientists throughout Stuart times and as a result some very exciting discoveries were made.

By the end of the period more was known about the human body, nature and the planets than ever before, although not everyone believed these new ideas. Charles II also took a keen interest in science. He founded a club called the Royal Society, where leading doctors, scientists and astronomers could discuss their work.

In 1628 William Harvey wrote a book explaining how the heart is a pump for moving blood around the body. Many people thought he was mad. It is said that in 1665 Isaac Newton discovered the law of gravity by watching an apple fall from a tree. He went on to put forward other important ideas about motion. Much of modern science is based on his ideas.

Sir Isaac Newton

James II

When Charles II died in 1685, his brother succeeded him and became King James II. He was a Catholic and soon began to put Catholics in positions of power in the army and government. This worried many leading Protestants and when James had a son to start a line of Catholic kings, they decided to make sure this would not happen.

They offered the crown to Mary, James's Protestant daughter and her husband William, the Dutch Protestant leader. William and Mary landed at Torbay and James marched to attack them. When his army and his generals began to desert, James lost the will to fight and fled to France. Parliament offered the throne jointly to William and Mary.

James fled by boat. He threw the 'great seal' into the Thames hoping that William and Mary would have problems ruling without it

Colonies and Trade

Throughout the Stuart period, the eastern coast of
America was settled by the British. The early pioneers
had a very hard time but eventually they set up
colonies which prospered through fishing, fur trapping
and tobacco growing.

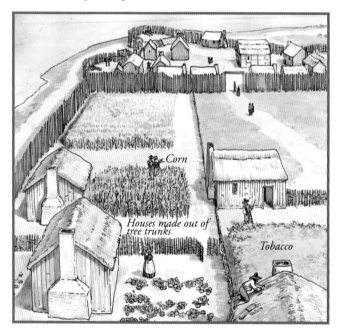

Corn

Houses made out of tree trunks

Tobacco

British ships traded all over the world, bringing back
goods such as sugar and indigo from the West Indies.
People put money into trading companies, like the East
India Company, sure that they would make big profits.

The Last of the Stuarts

When William and Mary came to the throne in 1689 Parliament drew up a list of rules to control their power. This list was called the Bill of Rights. When William signed the Bill, Parliament finally won the great struggle which had gone on throughout the Stuart period to decide whether Parliament or the monarch was more powerful.

Bill of Rights - 1689
1. Parliament will decide on all laws and taxes.
2. The King must be a Protestant.
3. No one can go to prison without a trial.
4. Parliament will decide on whether there will be an army.

When William died in 1702, James II's other daughter Anne became queen. During her reign Members of Parliament began to divide into two parties, the Whigs and the Tories. In 1707 England and Scotland united and the two countries were talked about as Great Britain.

Queen Anne and her ministers

THE LADYBIRD BOOK OF

BRITISH

HISTORY

The Georgians

1714–1830

The Four Georges

Queen Anne had no children that lived, so when she died in 1714 Parliament offered the crown to a German prince, George of Hanover, the great-grandson of James I. He became George I. He spoke no English, and he was unpopular for much of his reign as were the three King Georges who followed him.

George I and George II both spent a lot of time in Germany and allowed a cabinet of powerful MPs to make most of the decisions for them. This group was led for many years by Sir Robert Walpole, who became Britain's first Prime Minister.

George III was a good family man but was not a skilled politician. He felt many MPs were dishonest and tried to rule more fairly by building up a party of friends in Parliament. He was not, however, very successful and during his reign Britain lost the American colonies. George was more interested in farming and encouraged many improvements in agriculture. He was called 'Farmer George'. During the later years of his reign he went mad.

George IV led a very wild life and was mainly interested in enjoying himself. His behaviour made him very unpopular with the British people.

George I

During the Georgian Age Britain became a great power. Although America was lost, Britain won Canada and India, laying the foundations for a great empire. The government, which was controlled mainly by rich merchants and large landowners, became strong and stable.

The first iron bridge

There were great changes in the countryside as farms were modernised, farming methods improved and rich landowners built magnificent houses set in splendid parks. Many of these stately homes still exist and can be visited today. Towns grew as the Industrial Revolution began and trade boomed. Some of the new inventions of the Georgian Age were: steam engines, flush lavatories, gas lighting, hot air balloons, buses and Braille.

Stephenson's Rocket   *Gas lighting*

Buses

Bonnie Prince Charlie

Prince Charles Edward was the handsome, ambitious grandson of James II known as Bonnie Prince Charlie. He believed that the crown should be returned to the Stuarts. In 1745 he landed in Scotland with French support to raise an army among the clans and gain the throne. After an early victory at the battle of Prestonpans, he invaded England. When he found that few English people supported him Charles retreated and went back to the Highlands of Scotland. He was pursued by George II's son, the Duke of Cumberland. At Culloden, near Inverness, the tired clansmen were at last defeated. A reward of £30,000 was put on Charles' head, but he hid and later escaped abroad.

The battle of Culloden

Charles was helped to escape by Flora Macdonald

Smuggling

During Georgian times British ships traded all over the world. They carried industrial goods to Europe, the Americas and India, and brought back luxuries like silk, sugar, tea, brandy and tobacco. Many people, especially along the south coast, turned to smuggling to avoid paying taxes on these expensive luxuries. However, smugglers could be hanged or transported (to the colonies) if they were caught by Customs men.

Smugglers, who were often fishermen, took cargoes from foreign ships, then brought them ashore secretly. Cargoes were hidden until they could be safely sold. Barrels of brandy might be towed behind the smuggling boat. If it was stopped the barrels would sink out of sight. Many smuggling boats had false bottoms where the cargo could be hidden and then covered with fish.

Shipwrecks were looted and sometimes whole villages shared in the profits from the stolen goods.

Wolfe and Quebec

In 1756, during the reign of George II, war broke out with the French in Canada. Both sides wanted to control the land and the rich fur trade there. As long as the French occupied the powerful fortress of Quebec they threatened the British colonies in America.

General James Wolfe was sent to capture the fortress of Quebec. The task seemed impossible as

there was no way up the steep cliffs on which Quebec stood. Wolfe spotted a narrow path leading up to the plain behind the city and led his soldiers up it. The whole British army crept up the narrow path to the Heights of Abraham behind Quebec during the night. They tricked the enemy sentries by answering their challenges in French.

Seeing the British in position the French General Montcalm led out his soldiers. The British waited until the French were very close, then fired. The French were beaten but Wolfe was killed in the battle. Quebec surrendered and Canada became a British colony.

The Loss of America

During the reign of George III the thirteen British colonies in America declared their independence from Britain. The colonists hated paying new taxes on goods like sugar, tea and paper. Many Americans felt no loyalty to a king who was 4,800 kilometres (3,000 miles) away and never visited America.

Although George III sent an army to put down the rebellion the Americans, led by George Washington and helped by the French, eventually forced the British to surrender at Yorktown in 1781. A new country, the United States of America, was born with Washington as its first President.

The Industrial Revolution

During the Georgian period, trade, industry and towns became much more important. This change, now called the Industrial Revolution, altered the ways in which people lived and worked.

The main change that took place was a result of the invention of machines to do work that used to be done by hand, as in the cloth making industry. These machines, driven at first by water and steam, were so large that they had to be put into special buildings. This meant that many cloth workers started to work in factories instead of at home.

Probably the single most important invention of the Industrial Revolution was the steam engine. This was used to drive the machines in the factories, to pump floodwater out of the mines and to power steam ships, among other things. Steam engines on wheels became the first railway locomotives.

Children sat for hours in the dark waiting to open the trap door

Young women dragged the coal along the tunnels

Wooden pit props held up the roof

As the Industrial Revolution got under way, more iron of a better quality was needed. For centuries iron smelting had been done with charcoal, but as wood became scarce, iron makers began to use coal instead. It was Abraham Derby who showed how coal baked into coke could be used to smelt iron.

Miners often had to lie on their sides to dig out the coal

The coal had to be carried up long ladders to the surface

Coal was already used to heat homes and in the brick making and beer brewing industries. Since most of the coal near the surface had been used up, miners had to dig much deeper to get the extra coal needed for the growing population and the new industries.

Crime and Punishment

Crime was very common in Georgian Britain. There was no proper police force so there were savage punishments for those who were caught, to put others off committing crimes.

The pillory was used for rogues and cheats who were often pelted by the crowd

In 1750 Henry Fielding set up the first detective force, later known as the Bow Street Runners. His blind brother, John, was a magistrate who was said to be able to recognise the voice of any criminal who had appeared before him.

There were over two hundred crimes for which the penalty was death. Huge crowds went to see public hangings like the ones at Tyburn, just outside London. There were often stalls and side shows as well.

Prisons were dirty and overcrowded. Murderers, lunatics, debtors and children were all mixed together in dreadful conditions. Typhus, or 'jail fever', killed a lot of prisoners. Some people, like John Howard, a magistrate, tried to improve conditions but it took over fifty years to replace all the old, unhealthy prisons.

A prison hulk. Many convicted criminals were kept in old ships like this before being transported to prison camps in Australia

Medicine

During the Georgian period the population of Britain more than doubled. This was partly because doctors were beginning to learn more about how to treat diseases. Over one hundred and fifty new hospitals were built. Operations were still dangerous. Surgeons had to work fast because there were no anaesthetics. Most of their patients died in agony of shock, or through infection because there were no antiseptics.

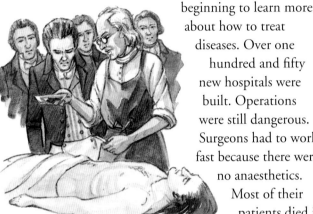

Medical students learned about the human body by dissecting the bodies of hanged criminals

In 1796 Dr Edward Jenner discovered that milkmaids who caught cowpox never caught smallpox, a disease that killed many children and scarred thousands of others. He vaccinated people with a mild dose of cowpox which protected them from the killer smallpox disease.

The need for more corpses led to an increase in the dreadful crime of bodysnatching

Daily Life

During the Industrial Revolution people moved from the countryside into the towns. The poor workers lived in tiny houses, often built by factory owners. The richer people lived in new, elegant terraces. Houses had to be built in four styles or 'rates' by law. The biggest was a first rate house which would be five storeys high and three windows wide.

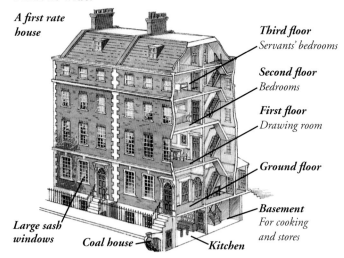

A first rate house

Third floor
Servants' bedrooms

Second floor
Bedrooms

First floor
Drawing room

Ground floor

Basement
For cooking and stores

Large sash windows

Coal house

Kitchen

Food was very plain for poor people, mainly consisting of bread with cheese or butter. Cheap meat was made into broth. Vegetables like carrots, parsnips and cauliflowers were eaten. The rich ate many different kinds of meat, especially beef and mutton, as well as fish and game. They also drank fine wines, but ale was the main drink of the poor.

Georgian men's clothes became simpler and less
colourful than the clothes of Stuart times. Gentlemen wore
long coats with high collars that were usually worn open.
Long waistcoats, knee length breeches, powdered wigs and
three-cornered hats were popular. By late Georgian times
men wore clothes based on riding costume.

*Hat and coat based
on French uniform*

About 1810

Silk bonnet

Hair in ringlets

Top hat

Tail coat

A dandy

*Tight
trousers*

Riding boots

Ladies wore full skirts
and petticoats stretched
over hoops. By the end
of the period dresses were
simpler and made of flimsy
see-through material, with very
high waistlines.

Captain Cook and Australia

Captain James Cook was one of Britain's greatest sailors. He was given command of the three great voyages of exploration round the world and visited many lands that no European had ever seen before. He took scientists with him

Cook's ship the Endeavour

so that they could study the plants and animals. Cook persuaded his sailors to eat pickled cabbage. As a result none of them suffered from scurvy, a disease that usually killed many sailors on long voyages.

Cook visited New Zealand and was the first European to land on the coast of Eastern Australia. He called the landing spot 'Botany Bay'. After 1788 Botany Bay became a prison settlement and shiploads of convicts were sent there. Settlers soon followed to set up farms. This threatened the way of life of the Australian Aborigines who lived by hunting.

The Slave Trade

The owners of sugar plantations in the West Indies, and tobacco and cotton farms in America wanted workers. British merchants soon found that they could make huge profits by carrying slaves from Africa to America.

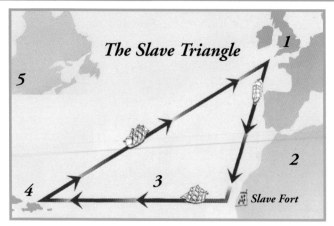

The Slave Triangle

1. **Britain**
Ships were loaded with cheap goods like knives, cloth, pots and pans to pay for the slaves

2. **Africa**
Slaves were captured by slavers and kept in forts until the ships arrived

3. **The middle passage**
The slaves were branded, packed onto the ships and chained in the holds. Many died on the long voyage west from disease or lack of water. The slavers were very cruel

4. **The West Indies** *and* 5. **America**
The slaves were auctioned and taken away by their new owners. They were very badly treated. Ships were loaded with sugar, molasses and rum which fetched high prices in Britain

William Wilberforce started a society in 1787 to abolish the slave trade. The plantation owners, who did not want to lose their cheap labour, fought this bitterly. However, Parliament slowly realised how terrible slavery was, and passed a law abolishing the British slave trade in 1807. Slavery in the British colonies was not abolished until 1833.

The Press Gang

Britain had only a small army because, as an island, her real strength lay in the Royal Navy. The Navy guarded the British Isles and protected British trade routes abroad. However, life in the Navy was hard and most men did not want to join up.

Naval captains sent press gangs ashore to find sailors. Likely men were made drunk or knocked unconscious, then dragged on board. When naval ships visited a port, the men who lived there would often hide or run away, because they knew that once they were in the Navy they might never see their families again. Sailors who broke the strict rules on board the ship could be flogged with a whip called a cat o' nine tails.

Nelson and Trafalgar

In 1805 the French emperor, Napoleon Bonaparte, had conquered most of Europe. He gathered a huge army at Boulogne and prepared to cross the Channel to invade Britain. Only the British fleet, led by Admiral Horatio Nelson, could save the country.

Nelson knew that if he could destroy the French fleet, the invasion barges would not dare to sail. He attacked the French navy off the coast of southern Spain near Cape Trafalgar. The battle was a great British victory and, although Nelson was killed, Napoleon had to call off his invasion.

Wellington and Waterloo

In 1815 Napoleon, who had been defeated by an alliance of Britain and the other European countries, escaped from his prison on the island of Elba off the west coast of Italy. When he reached France Napoleon quickly raised another army.

He attacked a small British army led by the Duke of Wellington near the village of Waterloo in Belgium. Wellington knew that if he held out until the Prussian army arrived victory would be certain.

At Waterloo the British formed into squares and fired rapid volleys into the French cavalry. Not even Napoleon's famous Imperial Guard could break the British ranks. Napoleon was defeated.

Wellington had been in the thick of the fighting on his famous horse Copenhagen. After his victory he was greeted in Britain as a national hero and later became Prime Minister.

THE LADYBIRD BOOK OF

BRITISH

HISTORY

The Victorians

1830–1901

Victoria and Albert

Princess Victoria was brought up very strictly. She was not allowed to speak to adults unless her governess was present. She could not read a book without permission.

After Victoria became queen at the age of eighteen this all changed. She had to talk to the Prime Minister and to read and sign important state papers.

Three years later Victoria married a German prince, Albert. They adored each other and they had nine children. Albert became his wife's closest adviser. When he died, after twenty-one years of marriage, Victoria went into mourning for years. She wore black, was rarely seen in public and became known as the 'Widow of Windsor'.

Victoria reigned longer than any other British monarch. Late in her reign Victoria became the ruler of many lands as the British Empire grew. She was called Empress of India. In 1887, huge crowds celebrated the Golden Jubilee which marked her fiftieth anniversary as queen.

Gladstone and Disraeli

William Gladstone and Benjamin Disraeli were the two most famous Prime Ministers in Victorian England. Gladstone was the leader of the Liberal Party and Disraeli was the leader of the Conservative Party.

They were both brilliant speakers who could inspire their audiences and they were both great reformers. But these two great statesmen had very different ideas and they detested each other. They became great rivals who dominated Victorian politics for nearly fifty years.

Gladstone had a strong sense of right and wrong and believed people should be judged on their merits, not their wealth. He supported the right of small nations, including Ireland, to govern themselves.

The witty Disraeli was an author as well as a politician. He wore fancy clothes and loved to poke fun at the serious-minded Gladstone. Disraeli was a strong supporter of the British Empire. He bought control of the Suez Canal and made Queen Victoria Empress of India.

At election time, both party leaders travelled around the country drumming up support. Gladstone could deliver a speech to thousands of people in the open air with his great booming voice.

Charity

Christianity had an important influence on Victorian society. Religion affected every aspect of people's lives. It encouraged people to provide charity at home and be missionaries abroad. In 1851, sixty per cent of people in Britain attended church.

William Booth, a Methodist minister, founded the Salvation Army in 1878 to preach and give help, shelter and food to the very poorest people. Another Victorian man called Dr Barnado devoted himself to the care of homeless children. His Barnado's Homes took in, fed, clothed and educated tens of thousands of poor children.

Most poor people were helped by private charity, mainly given by the church. A new system of poor relief, called the Poor Law, was introduced in 1834. All those who needed help, such as orphans, the sick, the old and unemployed, had to go into a workhouse.

In the workhouse, conditions were deliberately harsh so that only those in real need would enter. Families were often split up, with males and females being separated. The inmates received a bare minimum of food and clothing. In return they had to do hard, boring work and obey strict rules. People were shocked by the descriptions of workhouse life in Charles Dickens' book, *Oliver Twist*.

Conditions in Factories

During the 1800s the Industrial Revolution continued throughout Britain. The use of new machinery led to a huge increase in the number of factories. Many factory workers were children. They worked long hours and were often treated harshly by the overseers. The first factory laws which laid down rules about pay and working conditions were not very effective. There were few factory inspectors to make sure the laws were obeyed. Many machines did not have safety guards and accidents were common.

Children continued to work in factories until 1880 when the introduction of compulsory schooling for children aged between five and ten helped to end child labour. There were other horrible jobs for children too. Small boys were sent up chimneys to sweep them by hand until a law in 1875 banned this.

Trade Unions

As more people came to work in factories, mills and mines, they began to group together to form trade unions. Most employers and the government disliked unions because they forced up wages and encouraged employees to protest about their working conditions.

Trade unions grew in spite of this opposition. Skilled workers such as engineers and coal miners formed unions which provided benefits for their members such as sickness and unemployment pay. The union movement spread to less skilled workers on the docks and in transport until about a quarter of all workers - men and women - were members of unions.

Many early unions met in pubs which came to be named after them. They discussed sickness benefits, pay and hours of work

The Co-operative Movement

Another way in which the workers tried to help themselves was through the Co-operative movement. This started when twenty-eight weavers opened a grocery store in Toad Lane in the Lancashire mill town of Rochdale in 1844. Each weaver put in one pound to buy household goods. These were sold to customers at fair prices. Each customer also received a dividend (a share of the profits) according to how much he or she had bought. At the end of the year the profits were shared out to the dividend holders. They could either spend their dividend or leave the money in the business as an investment on which interest would be paid.

The shop in Rochdale was so successful that similar 'Co-ops' sprang up in other towns. At this time, food was often impure and goods were poor quality. The Co-ops provided good quality food, clothes and goods at reasonable prices. They also gave people the chance to save.

The Chartists

In 1836 only one male in forty was allowed to vote. Many working class men were angry that they could not vote. They organised a campaign to make voting fairer by collecting signatures for a huge petition, or charter. They became known as the Chartists.

Parliament refused to take any notice of the charter, and Chartist leaders were imprisoned. Eventually the movement died out. Even so, by 1918 nearly all of the aims of the charter had been achieved. Today, everyone over the age of 18 has the right to vote.

The demands of the Chartists
1. *All men over twenty-one to be allowed to vote*
2. *All voting to be secret*
3. *All voting areas to be the same size*
4. *MPs to be paid*
5. *People to be allowed to become MPs without being landowners*
6. *A new Parliament to be elected every year*

Schools

During Victoria's reign a system of elementary education for all children was developed by the Church. After 1870 the government, realising that a well-educated workforce was necessary to run the machines and factories of Britain, played an important part in providing the extra money needed to improve education. Schooling became free in 1891. Then, in 1899, the school leaving age was raised to twelve.

Railways and Steam Ships

Railway travel transformed people's lives. Trains were first designed to carry goods but soon passengers, especially from the working classes, began to travel by rail. Cheap Day Excursion trains became popular, and seaside resorts grew rapidly. Between 1835 and 1865 about 25,000 kilometres of track were built, and over 100 railway companies were created. Railways even changed the time. The need to run the railways on time meant that 'local time' was abolished and clocks showed the same time all over the country.

From 1843 onwards larger steamships started to be built with iron, and later steel. The invention of screw propellers, steam turbine engines, oil and diesel engines, and the building of coaling stations along the trade routes, made steamships much more efficient.

The Exhibition building was nicknamed the
Crystal Palace. It was destroyed by fire in 1936

The Great Exhibition

In 1851 Prince Albert planned a Great Exhibition to
celebrate the achievements of British and foreign
industry. The Exhibition was housed in a startling
new building made of iron and glass which was put up
in Hyde Park, London.

The Exhibition was a huge success with over 7,000
British exhibitors and 6,000 from abroad. There were
over six million visitors, many of whom came on
special cheap trains. The Exhibition showed the strength
of British industry. For the next twenty years Britain
was known as the 'workshop of the world'. During the
twenty-six weeks of the Exhibition the visitors drank one
million bottles of mineral water.

The Crimean War

In 1854 Britain and France went to war in the Crimea to support Turkey against Russia. The war was badly organised. The British soldiers were poorly equipped and before long, dysentery and cholera were sweeping through their ranks.

The Charge of the Light Brigade

The Charge of the Light Brigade was one of the biggest disasters of the war. Out of the 673 men who made the charge, only fifty stayed in their saddles, 113 were killed, and many more were wounded – all the result of a mix-up in orders.

Florence Nightingale was sent to the Crimea with thirty-eight nurses. She organised the cleaning of the filthy hospital at Scutari, and brought in proper nursing. The death rate fell dramatically. She was called 'the lady with the lamp' because every night she toured the wards comforting the soldiers.

The Indian Mutiny

In 1857 British rule in India was threatened by a mutiny of the sepoys in the army of the East India Company. The sepoys refused to use gun cartridges which had been greased with beef and pork fat. Because of their religious beliefs, Hindus refused to touch beef and Muslims refused to touch pork. This sparked off a great rebellion which swept through much of India. Many Indians, both rich and poor, resented British rule which they felt threatened their traditional way of life. There was savage fighting by both sides before British rule was restored.

After the mutiny Victoria became Empress of India and the country was put under the direct rule of a British Viceroy. The Indian princes gave their loyalty to the Crown.

Under the rule of the Raj roads, railways and postal services were set up. In return India provided a market for British goods and a supply of men for British colonial armies.

India became known as the 'Jewel in the Crown' of Queen Victoria.

The Zulu War

British soldiers were fighting a war somewhere in the vast British Empire during every single year of Queen Victoria's reign. One of the fiercest struggles was against the Zulus in South Africa. The Zulus were a very warlike people. Boys were trained to fight and all Zulu men were warriors. A Zulu army could run all day then fight a battle in the evening.

In January 1879 a British army invaded Zululand. Part of the army was attacked by over 20,000 Zulus at Isandlwana. The British force of 1,500 men was massacred. Shortly after this disaster, fewer than 200 soldiers – many of them wounded – held off a force of 4,000 Zulus which attacked them at Rorke's drift. The British fired over 20,000 bullets.

In July 1879 the British army destroyed Ulundi the Zulu capital. Cetshwayo, the Zulu king, was captured and the power of the Zulu army was broken.

Cholera

In Victorian times there was no efficient rubbish collection or sewage disposal, so water supplies were often polluted. Town privies were shared by several families. Many people collected all their water from public water pumps. Pollution seeping into the water from nearby privies, dung heaps and rubbish piles caused diseases which spread like wildfire through the crowded slums. Epidemics of killer diseases, such as typhoid and cholera, persuaded the government to take action by passing laws to improve water supplies, sewage disposal and housing. This led to a great improvement in health and living conditions in towns.

Daily Life

Before 1850 the diet of poor people was mainly made up of bread and dripping. As the Industrial Revolution took place, factories started to mass-produce foods. Canned foods were sold for the first time, which brought a greater variety to people's diets. Refrigerators were invented which meant that food sold in shops was fresher.

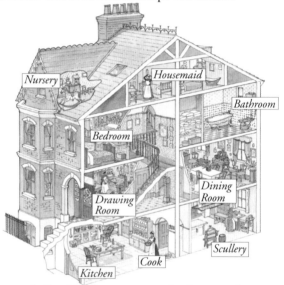

Many people lived in slums near to the factory where they worked. These were small, badly built terraced houses, which were cramped and filthy.

Middle class people moved out of the cities into new, cleaner suburbs. The houses here were large and strongly built. The Victorians loved to fill their houses with ornaments and decorations.

During the first forty years of Victoria's reign, women wore huge skirts and many petticoats. These layers were supported by a stiff wire cage called a crinoline. Men dressed in frock coats, waistcoats and trousers. Women wore strong corsets stiffened with whalebone or steel. These were laced very tightly to give them tiny waists. Corsets were very unhealthy because they stopped the wearer breathing properly.

A woman about 1855

Poor people often bought second-hand clothes

Side whiskers

Lace collar

Scarf instead of a tie

Jacket with slit sleeves

Starched cravat

Boots

Underfoot straps

No shoes

Corset

A gentleman about 1850

By the end of the century women's skirts had become much tighter and bell-shaped. Baggy trousers, called bloomers, became fashionable as women's sportswear.

The End of the Victorian Age

In 1897 a Diamond Jubilee was held to celebrate Queen Victoria's sixtieth year on the throne. Representatives came from all over the Empire to pay their respects. But the queen's health was already failing. She spent much of her time in a wheelchair. During the last four years of her reign, she became increasingly ill and depressed.

She died on 22 January 1901. All over Britain people went into mourning. Thousands of people went to her funeral. Many wept in the streets as her coffin passed. She was buried beside her beloved Albert, the man she had loved and mourned so long.

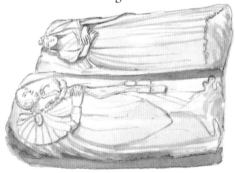

The tomb of Victoria and Albert at Frogmore

THE LADYBIRD BOOK OF

BRITISH
HISTORY

The War Years

1901–1945

The Edwardian Age

In 1901 Queen Victoria's son became King Edward VII. He was already sixty years old. The easy-going Edward was very different from his serious-minded mother. He loved ceremonies, banquets, gambling, going to the races and visiting the theatre. The years that Edward was king are called the Edwardian Age. This was a time of great change. Cars and aeroplanes became popular among the very rich. Old age pensions were started. Women demonstrated for the right to vote. Modern Britain had arrived.

King Edward VII was known as 'Bertie'. He had never been allowed to play a great role in public affairs by his mother. He preferred pleasure to study and spent much of his time as Prince of Wales enjoying himself.

Edward VII attended the 1908 Olympic Games that were held in London

Suffragettes

During the Edwardian Age more women began to demand the right to vote. Suffragettes organised petitions to Parliament, held public meetings and marched with banners in the street. When Parliament would not listen they used more violent methods. They smashed shop windows, set fire to letter boxes and attacked government ministers. Many went to prison where they went on hunger strikes and were brutally fed by force. The suffragette movement was led by Mrs Emmeline Pankhurst and her two daughters.

A suffragette demonstration

Reform

At the start of the twentieth century Britain was one of the richest and most powerful nations in the world. But many of her people were very poor.

The Liberal government, which included David Lloyd George and Winston Churchill, came to power in 1906. It brought in some important reforms.

- Pensions for people over seventy years old
- A National Insurance scheme to help people who missed work through illness
- Labour exchanges to help people to find jobs
- A weekly sum of money (called benefit) paid to unemployed men in certain trades
- Minimum wages for some low paid workers
- Free school meals for some needy children

The government had to fight hard to bring about these changes. Many people still believed, like the Victorians, that poor people should be helped only by private charity. Now the government recognised that it had a duty to help those in need.

The National Insurance Act was introduced, which meant that the workers, the employers and the state each paid a certain amount of money per week. In return, workers could claim money if they became ill.

In large cities, such as London and Glasgow, many poor families lived in slums

World War I

When Germany invaded Belgium in 1914 World War I began. Thousands of young men volunteered to join the army, believing the war would be an exciting adventure and their patriotic duty.

Most British soldiers fought on the Western Front in France. They lived in trenches dug in the ground. Between the two armies lay a wasteland known as 'no man's land', where exploding shells carved huge craters and the rain turned the earth to mud.

These soldiers are wearing masks to protect them from poison gas

Parapet of sandbags

Periscope to see over the parapet without being shot

The mud-filled trenches where British soldiers had to live were shaped like this to protect them from bomb blast. People who stayed at home knew little about the real horror of trench warfare but were shocked by the huge number of deaths.

Machine guns cut down attacking soldiers in their hundreds, but neither side was able to drive the other back, so the war dragged on until 1918. Nearly three-quarters of a million British soldiers, many just teenagers, were killed. Their names can be seen engraved on war memorials in towns and villages throughout the country.

Tanks were first used in 1916

Women in the War

As thousands of men went off to fight, their jobs were filled by women. Women soon proved that they were as good as men even in hard and dirty jobs such as farming, heaving coal and repairing motor vehicles. Many also did dangerous jobs such as working in munitions factories and being fire fighters. This war work helped women to win the right to vote. But they had to give most of their jobs back to the men returning from the war.

The General Strike

After the war some British industries found it hard to sell the goods they produced to foreign countries. The coal industry was badly affected. Coal mine owners decided to lower the price of their coal by cutting miners' wages. The miners would not accept this and called on other unions to join them in a General Strike which began on May 3rd 1926.

The miners demanded 'not a penny off the pay, not a minute on the day', but the government would not meet their demands. The union leaders called off the strike after only nine days. The miners continued to strike for another nine months. Hunger eventually drove them back to work on lower wages.

Although the regular trains and buses stopped, there were no ordinary newspapers and the docks were at a complete standstill, the nation did not come to a complete halt. Volunteers, such as students and professional workers, helped to keep things going by volunteering to drive buses and trains. Motorists gave people lifts to work. Volunteer bus drivers were protected by barbed wire and policemen.

Daily Life

Between the wars, estates of council houses were built in many towns to provide decent homes at a low rent. In spite of this there were still families living in overcrowded slums.

Women began to wear looser fitting, more comfortable dresses, and more make-up. During the war a lot of men were in the armed forces, and wore uniforms. When on leave they wore 'utility suits'. Clothes and fabric were rationed, so women had to make outfits from clothes or material they already had.

Ration Book

During both world wars, food was rationed. The amount of food that each person was allowed each week in 1941 is shown below. It doesn't look very much, but it was more than many poor people had been eating before the war.

Bread, potatoes, onions and carrots were not rationed

1 pint of milk, 56g of sugar, 2 eggs, 65g of tea, 110g of bacon, 28g of cheese, 5p's worth of meat, 56g of sweets, 56g of butter

World War II

In 1933 Adolf Hitler became leader of Germany. He built up German forces and marched into Austria in 1938 then Czechoslovakia in 1939. It was clear that Poland would be his next victim. Britain and France announced that they would protect Poland from attack.

On Friday September 1 1939 German forces invaded Poland. At quarter past eleven on the following Sunday morning, people huddled around their wireless sets to hear Neville Chamberlain, the Prime Minister, declare that Britain was at war with Germany. People began to prepare for air raids by German bombers.

Air raid wardens patrolled the towns giving out gas masks, checking that the blackout was complete and reporting any bomb damage to the rescue services

Over two million children were evacuated from the large towns to the countryside. The government provided Anderson shelters for people to build in their gardens.

The Battle of Britain

In 1940 the Germans invaded France. They drove back the British and French forces. The British army was trapped at Dunkirk. Thousands of small boats helped the Royal Navy to rescue them. Britain stood alone, waiting for a German invasion.

Throughout the summer of 1940 the Luftwaffe bombed British airfields, trying to destroy the Royal Air Force. Hitler thought that once the RAF was defeated, his armies could cross the Channel and invade.

Britain had effective defences
Radar stations and spotters detected attacking enemy planes

A picture of the attack was built up on a map table in the ops room. Plotters moved markers to show the position of German planes

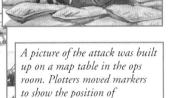

Information about the numbers, height, position and direction of attacking planes was sent by telephone or radio to Fighter Command

Officers at Fighter Command ordered the nearest squadron of fighters to scramble. Radio operators told the fighter pilots the position and height of the enemy planes, and the best direction from which to attack

The Blitz

German losses in the Battle of Britain were so great that in the middle of September 1940 they gave up attacking the RAF. They began to bomb British cities such as London, Coventry, Glasgow and Swansea instead.

Thousands of Londoners sheltered night after night in underground stations while bombs exploded on the ground above them. On the worst nights it seemed as if all London was ablaze. Gas, water and electricity were often cut off. Many people lost their families, homes and possessions. It was a terrible time, but the Blitz failed and Britain survived to win the war. Throughout this turbulent time, British people were encouraged by the strong leadership of Prime Minister Winston Churchill.

Victory

In 1941 the USSR and the USA joined the war on Britain's side. Slowly defeat turned into victory. German U-boats were beaten in the Battle of the Atlantic. The German army was defeated in Russia, North Africa and Italy.

On June 6 1944 (D-Day) after months of preparation, Allied troops landed on the beaches of Normandy in France. The Germans were slowly driven back to their borders. After months of bitter fighting, Germany surrendered in May 1945. The nightmare of war finally ended in August 1945 after the USA dropped the first atomic bombs.

Legacy

Towards the end of the war a Labour government was elected. It aimed to give jobs and homes to everyone. The National Health Service was set up so that anyone could see a doctor free of charge. Many council houses were built and children were able to go to school up to the age of fifteen.

The Depression and two world wars had exhausted Britain. The great overseas British Empire was about to disappear, and Britain was no longer a world leader. On the other hand, within ten years of the end of World War II, the British people were better fed, better housed, better educated and had more money to spend than ever before.

Medicine had taken great strides forward: immunisation, for example, meant that fewer babies died, and some diseases had almost disappeared. Advances in science had lifted Britain out of the steam age and into an age of electricity, cars and jet engines.

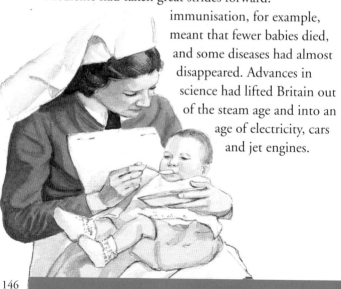

Glossary

Aborigines the original inhabitants of Australia

amphitheatre a circular or oval open-air theatre used for gladiator and animal fights

anaesthetics drugs used before an operation so that the patient feels no pain

Anderson shelters air raid shelters made from iron sheets which were covered with earth

antiseptic a liquid that stops a wound becoming infected

apprentice learner of a craft, being trained

bailiff lord of the manor's chief officer

Blitz short for Blitzkrieg (lightning war). The name given to the attack on British cities by German bombers during World War II

bodysnatching taking bodies from graves, usually for medical research

branding burning with a red-hot iron

Celts Iron Age tribes from Europe

civil war a war fought between the citizens of the same country

Commonwealth a state in which the whole people have a voice and an interest

courtier person at the royal court

dandy an elegant dresser

D-Day the day chosen for the invasion of German-occupied Europe

ealdormen powerful landowners

election choosing members of parliament by voting

empire several foreign countries ruled by another country

enclosure dividing the land and surrounding the new fields with hedges

Great Seal a stamp which was pressed onto hot wax to leave an impression. It was used to seal documents which were issued in the name of the monarch

house of correction where poor people were given food in exchange for work, and could be punished

hung, drawn and quartered a method of execution where criminals were first hanged, then had their vital organs removed and their bodies cut into four parts

jousting combat between two knights, on horseback

local time before 1852 the country had many different time zones. London time was eleven minutes ahead of Bristol time

Luftwaffe German air force

masterpiece finest piece of work

monastery a house where monks live and work

mutiny a rebellion of soldiers against their officers

noble person of high rank such as a lord

rationed shared out fairly

republic a country without a monarch that is ruled entirely by parliament

sepoys Indian soldiers who served in the East India Company's army

siege-engine a Roman machine used to capture a castle

treason treachery against your own country

vaccinate to protect a person from disease by giving them a small dose of a similar disease

Index

Timeline of
BRITISH
HISTORY

55BC–AD1945

55BC – Roman fleet appears off British coast
54BC – Julius Caesar lands in Britain

0

AD43 – Claudius invades Britain with his general Aulus Plautus. Most of England conquered in four years

60 – The Iceni tribe, led by Boudicca, revolts, burns London and is then defeated
The Brigantes tribe is conquered
Wales is conquered and many legionary forts are built there

200 – Hadrian's wall rebuilt. Romans attack Scotland again and Scottish tribes surrender. Britain divided into two provinces

0

Scotland is abandoned by the Romans – **100**

The Emperor Hadrian visits Britain – **122**
Hadrian's wall is begun

Saxon pirates raid the south coast – **250**